Venus & Don Juan

CAROL FROST

TRIQUARTERLY BOOKS
NORTHWESTERN UNIVERSITY PRESS

Evanston, Illinois

TriQuarterly Books
Northwestern University Press
Evanston, Illinois 60208-4210

Printed in the United States of America

ISBN 0-8101-5062-X (CLOTH)
ISBN 0-8101-5063-8 (PAPER)

Library of Congress Cataloging-in-Publication Data

Frost, Carol, 1948–
    Venus & Don Juan / Carol Frost.
        p.   cm.
    ISBN 0-8101-5062-X (alk. paper). —
    ISBN 0-8101-5063-8 (pbk. : alk. paper)
    I. Title
    PS3556.R596V46 1996
    811'.54—dc20   96-23430
                                    CIP

For David Svahn and David Vaules

White, through white cities passed on to assume
That world which comes to each of us alone.
"For the Marriage of Faustus and Helen," Hart Crane

We can evade you and all else but the heart.
What blame to us if the heart live on.
"Chaplinesque," Hart Crane

If any beings felt emotions of benevolence toward me, I should return them an hundred
and an hundred fold: for that one creature's sake, I would make peace with the whole kind.
Frankenstein, **Mary Shelley**

Elle ne concevait pas qu'aimer fût l'ennemi d'aimer.
Sainte-Beuve

Contents

Acknowledgments

The author wishes to thank the editors of the publications where many of these poems first appeared:

American Poetry Review, "Joy"
The American Voice, "Failure"
Crazyhorse, "Consent"
Gettysburg Review, "Farewell to Two Muses," "Former Beaus," "Morphine"
Green Mountain Review, "Denial," "Heart"
Indiana Review, "Adultery," "Lies"
North Dakota Review, "Envy," "Help"
One Art, "Craving," "Ecstasy"
Pivot, "Abstraction"
Ploughshares, "Companion Of," "Bliss," "Self"
Prairie Schooner, "Hypocrisy"
Shenandoah, "Imagination"
The Southern Review, "Custom," "Sex," "Scorn"
Third Coast, "Prodigal"
TriQuarterly, "Conscience," "Brave," "Obsession," "Patience," "Comfort"
Volt, "Pity," "Compatibility"

"Scorn" also appeared in *The 1995–1996 Pushcart Prize Anthology* (Pushcart Press, 1996).

Thanks to the National Endowment for the Arts Foundation for their support.

One

Companion Of

And yet this great wink of eternity

October was what it had already become when I entered the walled graveyard,
    the air golden and remote
in the last minutes before evening. A bedstand and springs made the gate,
    pulled aside,
and the stones faced the sunset, all those not overturned, flung like cards
from the losing player's hand. How long the dead had lain listening, looking back,
was written on their markers—granite, sandstone, slate—also marriages, loves
    ("companion of"),
homely avowals of affection cut in verse.
As day relented, I could have sworn there was no more reason than before for
    agony or joy,
that it had been outlived, except I saw one stone with the barest evidence of
    lettering—a staff with notes
unsounded, but felt. And I knelt to make out what I could and ran my hand as if
    over paper over the cool stone,
and I found under a cache of yellow, crumbling leaves the pried-off surface,
    broken by the years
in nine uneven pieces. What else was I meant to do for Mary Hyatt but take home
    the words for her?
Then it was impossible not to imagine her days and nights, especially her nights,
    when the air seems to suffer most
from all that has come and what is no longer likely to come. She enters the rooms I
    lend her,
humming a melody whose words she's nearly forgotten. How significant and
    strange the badly remembered air.
It gets in her blood, no forget-me-not gayer for the neck and face, and the absent
    lover is everywhere,
in the shadows, frost on the panes, a soliloquy over the piano or the card game.
Before bed, she writes him a letter.

The last time we met you had less and less to say, and though I felt I understood your private musings (oh, joys, memories of past experiences altogether your own, ghosts, guilts, pains), I felt my own words falling away from me. One quiet bred another. In the end, we forgot to say good-bye. Tell me next time we meet you'll read to me the lines of poetry you are so fond of, that I once heard you say with all the passion of youth, that so moved us both, though we are no longer young! Without the trouble of saying a thing meant, the meaning comes into suspicion. And if nothing is meant, the thing isn't worth recall. I think I know your thoughts but it is better to hear them from your mouth. I long for you.

He responds, and everything is as it was. Her cheeks burn and her hands tremble. For years.

Until chance, seedy and blind, ruins them; in the fresh dark there are no words left for this. It is better so.

Worse to hear it from human lips than in the clattering leaves—a rancid song—or in the night owl's scream.

Obsession

Never was life more nervous, sweeter, denser than nutmeat
and honey than when she was obsessed with who she was.
It was like passing between two mouths a morsel, thinking of swallowing later, if at
    all:
—Narcissus at daybreak rinsing his forehead and watching the beautiful tears.
If *he* stayed an eternity on his knees, why couldn't she?
But something interfered, asking her to weigh once more from the beginning
her gravity against her alibis:—the responsibilities—
till she put back the dividing walls inside her mind.
From time to time at night or when she walks alone in a summer field the
    delicious sense
still returns to her, God knows from where, and she believes she is different,
as if from a far-off world.

Imagination

Imagine that there are several paths. But none takes her
away. Whether she goes past the laid-up stones of the dam and a pent-up pond,
or into some foreign silent meadow with raspberry canes, she returns to the same
shaded entrance, as if she could never err, her mind won't let her.
Numbed and insane, she feels like someone's trapped stone
creature: a weather-beaten sylph holding onto a gate.
Why doesn't she just go, avoiding turns to the left and right,
until everything behind her is unfamiliar, unrelated; and she can be utterly new?
You may ask, but what do you know with your maps, books, and clocks? Stuck
as you are, will you yank off the silent dial face and, taking no counsel,
walk unfettered into the wild north fields?

Icarus in Winter

If Breughel was wrong, and Icarus fell in the dead of the year,
freezing in the stratosphere that made his wings' wax brittle,
he fell here where a ball of suet hangs from a string

like a little low earth. How lonesome evening seems,
as if something felt part of itself missing.

The people indoors watching television, sitting in chairs,
seem never to come into the yard; they do not lament
the season's decrease. They only feed the few birds.

Where are yesterday's sparrows and wrens?
Above the branches of the oak,
washed in colors we feel but cannot find?

Swan-colored, ice-colored, rare-gas-and-light-colored,
sounding to those indoors like a natural disaster—
a broken bough, a barn roof lost—Icarus

fell in this bare yard with no witness—no one
plowing a field, no ship of state concerned with itself,
no evidence of suffering.

                      These sightless walls
and shoveled entrances where no one comes,
even the white ground where Icarus is lying—

how sorrowless they make the landscape seem.
But no lie is made up entirely of lies,
and who knows who feels what and how much,

sickening at spectacle, turning off the TV.
Beneath the snow are pieces of every summer, buds and
stunted roots so far below sense they don't show.

Two

Heart

The Hapsburgs

Once we were inflamed as you, insatiate one,
as hot in the face, as empty-eyed and, centuries ago, also loved, slept, ate.
We shone so in our rubies and royal clothes, as you in a cotton shirt,
and in the beloved's presence were completely full and overflowing
or cold from her disinterest. Over and over we cradled ourselves
in our arms, and could feel the beloved grow weak and held her toward the bed.
We touched her with our lips . . . and through her swoon
the touch reached her deep within, under the breasts, until at last her inmost self
yielded.
          We shall not describe the last consummation,
or the last scent of possibility in the air
that went out the nostrils.
But there are jars in which these reflections lie as if drowned,
twisted into one intense shape, redolent, never to be annihilated.
Take heart. Take heart. Bring her to you.

Help

Vexing the water with its shadow, the heron told her where to fish,
and she did, thinking about the abject
tone of her brother's voice on the phone as if he no longer could believe in his own
   life.
She, though, as she cast and cast into the deep pool, hoped
he would grip himself and forget the woman who'd gone off with another man.
When she'd heard that he'd started drinking, she'd phoned him. He'd talked like
   someone
who had forgotten too much—: that a random stranger had destroyed him. He *was*
   in pieces,
and she wanted to help. But she wasn't sure she could bear to hear his voice again
that seemed to have been howling from the very first. As she stepped over the blue
   entrails of the trout
that lay on the gravel bed where the heron had been frightened, she looked up. No
   heron.
The sky neither questioned nor replied; its hard beauty lodged deep inside her.

Pity

When the woman falls in the garden and hurts her hand, all the blows
that have ever struck her, to which she had to yield, seem to return,
so morose the look in her eyes. But haven't they always been there,
saved up and partly concealed, so she could look them over one by one,
eating and sleeping with them? The blows
live in her honeycombed mind and newly with each passing day
establish what she will give away and what she will share.
As she holds her wrist, she waits for the tumult in her body to dwindle—
a blue welt is forming under a fingernail—and she breathes the summer air,
soft as skin on warm tomatoes. It is hard to believe in what goes on without one.
And the heart learns a pity for itself, easy, coarse, common as the grave.

Denial

Through smoked glass, as if he could shut out all worries, the great ones and the
    small ones,
the limousine driver sees the city (: more smoked glass and towering stone),
where children walk in high-top sneakers, and fevers fall
on others—the men in corners who shout at the empty space in front of their eyes.
They would gladly tell lies, or the interesting truth, he thinks,
if someone would listen, but all the denial
they've ever felt has stuck to them, flushed and dirty like skin.
Everyone hurries by. The man in the limousine
is paid to ride from doorway to doorway like a grand procession,
and if through the window lunatics flaunt themselves, life is like that—
as though somewhere above a god, or Pharaoh, with a face of absolute refusal, were
    turning away.

Bag Lady

Here is another parable in the mouth of a stranger:
on a city street, you will see her

as you walk to the opera—perhaps *La Bohème,*
or another romance where death becomes

the only way to solve the excesses
of love and forgiveness. Only the ignominious

and beautifully sung moments of dying have any meaning now,
unless the woman with her possessions and sorrow

rolled in a ball of cloth, plastic, and twine
says something about the heart as if it were yours or mine.

Virtuous she woke in the arms of the father
of her children. It was a kind of splendor

to wake in the spring light streaming through washed glass,
a hand stroking the small of her back or breast.

What did they think? What did they talk about?
It mattered, but they didn't know it.

Then came a change, the gingerly way he held her
a mimic gesture of support. Even the savior

of the world needed that.
Which heresy pretends he did not?

—Now seeing her as she is alone,
as she walks from dustbin to dustbin

talking to herself, listening to a roar, like water, in her ear
it seems we walk with her, if unseen, while past and future slide in a weir.

Her words cannot be heard above the traffic noises,
nor ours, and whose voice is

powerful enough to call down the old antagonist, who forsakes:—
the cloud-soft hand that enfolds us or breaks

the spirit? "Thou shalt not," she says, holding in her bundle, in grief
or pleasure, nothing: the nothing for which there is no preparation and no relief.

For R. K.

Craving

Don Giovanni

When the man in his dissolution enters the house and assaults a woman in the
    dark,
he's shocked, almost, to hear her cry for help, but his deceit is still rich and deep,
and he avenges himself with the point of a sword, killing the father,
hardening against reproaches, laughing at them, so he might go on lightly.
Only in the last night of life do they rise up and gaze on him.
When did he go too far? —weighing, in secret, his own weaknesses
against the world's beauty; comparing; until there was no end to it. The image of
    the father,
hers, even his, comes to ask him his worth. And we pity his lies, for the enormity
his will has seized on begins to take hold, reaching its tentacles through the room.
When it goes back to God it drags him with it, while he babbles,
still craving the women he never possessed and only pretended to make love to.

Lies

Isn't there a race of people made of glass, who when spilling
too much of themselves on someone's sofa, in someone's house, act shattered?
They have come to the party as if in someone else's place,
perjuring with too-little-allowed and agreeable nods themselves:
When they laugh with the general laughter, it's a queer, ceramic chiming.
Who invited them? It's as if, wanting to fit in, they would give promise after
    promise,
limitless and indistinct, and as if they were their own diaries no one must read
except for a few paragraphs which contain a modest wording for what is not mean-
    ingless
nor all lies. On timid feet they carry themselves through the knots of men and
    women—;
every voice's tone is as if to be avoided, as if cold every other person's bearing—;
until one of their great sorrows falls from their lips. And then apology.

Conscience

The crow settles on a fir bough and disappears
(the way a guard waits by the threshold to the Old Dutch Masters' room
and watches. What does he think?). Not even the hunters and the dogs
are reminders the crow exists, and it would seem he would never come back,
reuniting with others in the winter sky and moving off,
until he does. A caw falls like a reprimand from his beak, and he emerges in his
     uniform black,
his wings trembling stiffly with their free ends. It is hard not to feel anger
at his assertion—how one feels life's unfairness, and little to help us in our hard
     choices.
What use the silence, semblance, and austere flying?
As the deep woods tower above, full of shapes, and the heavens threaten snow,
something is moving near as if it wanted to tear us from our molds:—as a con-
     science is torn.

Three

Envy

Look: the cat lifts its head, switching its tail, and to the other cat says
in a voice almost too low to hear, something angry, interrupting their shared meal.
Hissing, they both stand absolutely
still—quivering, full of mistrust—equally, it seems, over the bowl with its sweet
    morsels
of flesh, though one must start to feel the other's resolve greater than her own;
or the other fetches from within a hardness like a beautiful blade
from a locked cabinet; because the first breaks away and walks to the other side
of the room. While the other's eating recommences, she springs onto the
    pampered chair
and sits looking out the window at the birds flitting by, if cat eyes don't blur
at that distance, then suddenly turns her head down to her chest
in a burst of envy to lick and lick her own fur.

Custom

As if it had forgotten everything—hatred, vindictiveness, the meaning of pain—
the bull took the ribboned sticks in his back without response, turning away,
so that when the picador entered the ring, the crowd was making fun
of the country's breeders. If there was an ounce of dignity or strength in the
    animal,
the picador would have to find it with his pole, and he came on slowly
to probe the back and shoulders:—deeply, cruelly, like a king with a scepter.
The bull barely moved until the picador gambled all and sailed his beautiful hat
    into the air
above the lowered head. With that the bull's will broke and he rushed again and
    again
like a child, a superbly angry prince, at the horse's side. When it was over, the bull
and its retinue gone inside to the abattoir, the picador, as was the custom,
    reentered the ring.
The assembly roared—by his actions they knew they knew better who they were.

Crows

Not disputing what those nearest her would think, their questions and
importunings, she goes out just after sunrise
into the morning green of the grassy earth, her nightgown soft around her legs, the
gun cradled lightly across her forearms.
The crows which have waked her lure her along—darkly a solitary shape flaring
through the naves of alder and beech,
the others calling. Those who have disturbed her sleep all month she means to kill,
for sleep is sacred, and private.
She has only to think this and she will return home, barefooted, and climb back
into bed.
The newspaper has not yet been delivered with its news of the world, the words
chanting violence and death, violence
in the face of disappointment, violence for no sake, and in her pure daze her
thoughts are more like this:
How far life reaches and where night and morning meet. From the mist a deer
walks suddenly into her field of vision,
and as suddenly she fetches from behind blinking lids a hardness, raising the .22 to
her shoulder and shooting it in the shoulder.
It falls, but when she leans into that remoteness—brown and still, its legs in the
air—it rolls to the right and springs away.
There is on her now what she can know only by violence. She can smell it (fur,
warmed earth, grass, blood) and hear it
in the raspings of the crows as she tries to follow the wounded buck:—what has
reposed all along in the part of her that isn't and is beast.

Four

Hypocrisy

Out of the same paints and objects that make up the bazaar around a cathedral—
cup, book, gold for embossing—comes the sacredness of the altar. And out of
    gestures
of those in the middle of sightseeing, walking and shifting packages
from one arm to another, emerges the one gesture
caught on the saint's face, a groaning for that which he feels he himself impedes.
How can he with so much want, the artist says, not surmount himself.
Disgust pulls around the mouth of the tourist and he leans against the stone
    balustrade.
He will only say he is tired and hot. Why doesn't everyone see the disfigurement
in his shoulders and face:—that his whole life is hypocrisy?
If they said what they meant, wouldn't each have to go on alone? So they start again
to peruse trinkets, pampering themselves with a drink and cake, liking the
    religious painting.

Joy

Ah, that Noah's joy lasted only for a time presses itself on the heart and mind.
When they called him foolish, he went on building.
But then among the drowned like soaking marionettes the ark bobbed, so that even
his closest friend meant *nothing* to the Father:—How could he hold onto his beliefs?
Like the caged beasts roaring, and as the wind beat itself on the water and the hull,
wouldn't he have liked to ease himself with yelling? Suddenly it comes to you:
he did yell. The trust he'd flung out with such abandon was absorbed by the gray pall.
And you harden yourself against the appearance of the landbird
—as if sunning his anguish and walking in washed and earth-spiced air
could rid the nostrils of the stench of the past forty days—,
a consummation that makes the sweat grow cold.

Consent

Arrows striking all sides of the body and St. Sebastian smiling—
his torso, the shoulder that flinches inadvertently, through the neck hole of his robe.
Suddenly he seems to have forgotten thirst, hate, fear of perishing,—consented,—
and the bowmen put down their bows.
Thus it has been. All were silent, but it was in his silence that the next morning
      came.
And they who'd shot him against their will,
who'd eaten and slept with others in the night and been utterly alone,
hoped he'd be gone,—his torn body under the soil. When they had him tied to a
      tree,
what did they have? standing full of memory, feeling the feathers scythe through
      the air,
displacing the sounds, trusting his god's descriptions as he leaned his head to
      his—
a little of what already exists and the towering sense of kindnesses no world can
      offer?

Morphine

for T. F.

Their single purpose was to ease her dying.
How much time did they think she was apt to have?—breath rasping,

eyes and lips raw as if she'd faced into an arctic storm,
then her voice reading from a last journal, lucid, firm—

not how much time was due her.
I hated them: the nurses checking oxygen levels, the doctor

smiling in deference to her weakening, and the four walls
and pillow keeping her through the night so carefully: loved, after all,

only her fidget for breathing,
a brief inhalation and the low, pursuing

exhale. Do you see? With death close-linked, we are made fools.
They could no more ease her anguish than heal

her—: On white paper are added another unit's
observations, the downward curve of vital signs, pen-prints

toward extinction. She lay motionless, then got the cold shivers
as they planned how much more morphine to give her.

—No lungs and voice left to do their own things,
all invaded, appropriated. I watched them bring

her in and out of coherence, destiny's hypnosis—
a long march through ice floes and extensive whiteness.

And they said she could feel herself strangle
but "wouldn't be aware or remember" the struggle.

We stood and watched. All around the halls fell silent,
time's suspended blank. Nighttime came and went.

And then death struck like an icy glove;
her face lost all its definition. No one moved.

Failure

I have come to fear
mornings when the night before has failed to stir through with fresh air
the small rooms where incidents I scarcely remember occurred:
The guilty lie on bedclothes, withdrawn, unclear about what to do, talking to
    themselves
until an uneasy sleep covers their eyes with gauze. Nor can I convalesce.
As if something pressed on the brain stem, there are bitter dreams. A life once
perhaps was spurned, a happiness turned down; I am loathed.
—Whatever was *done*, I have embarrassed my own heart and no longer see
in the mirror the child of nine whose brow and eyes are clear as a stand of birch
    in May,
who hasn't been orphaned or torn by what I myself may have invited,—
that darkly comes into the adult house and seems to want to nail closed the win-
    dows and doors.

Comfort

Because a sorrow was conquered, or a sin, can they relax?
No. Having felt hands crush and throw them down,
they see the ones in pieces everywhere and hear the eerie beat of their madness:
it trembles in the wings of hummingbirds, aloft as they eat, flying backward.
So they persist without knowing how, and having been forbidden
presence, to push and cajole the ones on their knees—in balls, in theirs and
    others' beds,
in hell—to their feet so they can find a way for themselves out into an airy place.
There they take down the hands flung before the face
and help to wash the inflamed portions of the others' hearts, so much like their
    own,
invisibly anointing whomever they can with oils, until and when the soft
pounding of their blood becomes comforting—like being held again in someone's
    arms.

Brave

                           That time, deaf to the entreaties of his parents,
Hector stood before the gates to meet Achilles: he hadn't yet admitted to himself
what would come to pass, supplicated his enemy for a clean grave;
like a lunatic when the angers that betrayed him suddenly unraveled,
grown stone-cold sane. The shivers took hold of him later—
breaker of horses, hard-hearted—and he ran. I think of this
as I talk to my friend, dead in his pants, phoning from his doctor's office
to reassure me, and when I walk with a woman who has learned her marrow
is too weak for another round of chemo. With clouds darkening
their shoulders, in mist—as hawk, as sunbeam—, the brave gods come, to beguile
    and taunt,
delivering a message, waiting for the response—*No use!*—, taking away what they
    came for.

Bliss

Hermes, so young, arrives to tell of spring,
a cold wind and a few feathers of snow accompanying him. His eloquences
are tinctured with yellow and reds—the first colors—
and he warms to his subject, remembering
an earlier year:—of the very sun's first ferment, of coltsfoot on the roads' verges,
of newnesses wherever the gods choose. And we listen, watching Hermes' feet
sink ankle-deep in the mud, a dog barking at someone, then a cry somewhere
    down the valley.
If the universe is cruel, we have grown used to it. Isn't there planting to take up,
the bearing and consequences to look forward to? We still might feel a precipitant
    hand
under the collar's nape and, more slowly, the bliss of holding,
like all creation, hyacinths, or another's face, up to lips, nostrils, eyes.

Five

Homo Sapiens

In this lonely, varying light of dawn with the residue of desire
like mist departing, I am walking. Was it in your eyes,
where my elongated face shone, I saw for the first time—
as if all the transparent fire in these trees had become palpable—
a hunger that was not wholly animal?
The need to tremble like dogwood, feeling the rain touch down.
My strange blood rises, and I may see you, fair leaves slipping over you, half-hidden
in the morning. With the beasts beside a pond,
I conjure the inward sun to leap into my brain. What remains?
Wild, beautiful petals all around.
A beast's face. And something, something else.

Compatibility

Never after was life so filled with meeting,
with reuniting and drawing apart as then, when bed-hot, filled with surges,
the man and woman began to know each other.
It was like the makeshift walking of geese toward water,—a settling into themselves
    and,
with a fiercer and fiercer grip, a testing of the untried other. How safe they'd been
    before
they touched and he asked her one thing which she meant to resist but was
    unable to.
How beautiful to keep one's fabled eyes closed:—Was another's body not like some
    bright
obstruction? But they, as if they knew nothing, opened entirely, bending to two wills,
striking down vanities, feeling what lay deep inside—the darker compatibilities—
until love seemed causal, not just related.
Their sinuous tongues used the word, over and over, without speaking.

Sex

If, as with a flock of sexless sheep, gently and without craving, apparently,
they walk beside each other for days, not pressing,—only let either's depth stir
and the other wants to soothe and understand. With fingers, elbows, breastbones.
One has had one's anger, one's faction, one's guarded place
no one can get into, least of all one so close;
yet who would believe the almost lethal force one wants to strike with sometimes,
as beasts hurt each other, biting, clamping onto the wounded neck.
What is any more potent and familiar? Wasn't she the one in whom
many times the other lost himself without reserve? Can he be in any other person
    more?
If Venus can be of little further assistance to this *pair,*
when she surges through the one, the other is dragged there—was, and will not go
    away.

Ecstasy

Her ecstasy rises like a rider on a leaping horse
and she knows to push through it calmly and completely, without rushing
or closing her eyes. The ground falls away, the sky, precipitate,
whirls about her shoulders, and she feels both saturated with motion and still.
If she thought (there is barely time), could it be of love's reciprocal
demands to give and be given?—as if an Angel appeared in the heart
and spoke: As your body rocks so shall his. So it seems,
because her hands, which were resting, dreamily
begin to stroke his neck and sides.
When she leans forward to whisper—a fondness and encouragement—
she is within herself again, exhilarated, and strangely proud.

Untitled

Remember the days of our arguing—
tempests, you called them, your tone wry, mocking;

so disruptive to our physical passion,
and enhancing. Our words struck to the marrow. When,

when, and whenever lust became love was the question.
The room we met in

was like an unforecasted island. Didn't you feel lost
in a way, and afraid? I tasted our sweat as it washed

over us and felt us moving toward our earliest natures—
what the bone frame (ribs and hips) is made for.

In an arboreal mist we knew the fever of the marrow,
greed churning and churning until it lets the other go.

We were alone and there were no appropriate words
afterward

or before.

Abstraction

In the heart a paper copy of a daguerreotype is fading and the body
of the beloved is palest yellow, disappearing from sight.
O that I might once more hear you speak and refuse you,
making of myself the lover who is drawn no longer toward the loved.
But the years! The years are severed into mists no farewell can alter,
not even the farewell that doesn't look or sound hurt. "Love is the enemy of love,"
you said, knowing I could not feel your hands, your breath on my throat,
and not try to comprehend, speaking in the abstract and superlative.
And, "The moon forgets us every morning."
That's how is was: a dark uncircumvented cool ending,
and how it is, already no longer really linked to me.

Adultery

Had she repented? Given over? No. She let others talk and pretended
to listen. It must be borne—commandment, moral—but not digested.
Jonah was not digested. And wasn't the inside of the snare sweet as ambergris some
    days?
She would not be another washed up on a shore, whose saving must be explained.
She would be with all the rest; for the rest: salt, tides, crying gulls, crabs,
the ones who catch crabs, the ones who kill those ones. These *were* her self,
and she would not purge herself. If her integrity was in question,
no one spoke of it, yet in company she was restrained, like one who in a moment
may say something coolly funny or devastating; until then holding a shell to her
    ear, to hear all
the singer hears, with hand pressed lightly to the ear—harmonies and the thrilling
unadulteration of her own notes, darkened perhaps with losses, sorrows, but still
    luring.

Patience

The man raises his eyes from the table and gazes at the murals of women
and can tell by the styling of their hair how long ago they were painted—
beautifully, seductively for the roomfuls of diners to come afterward.
So close, large in their pastel dresses, weren't they meant to be listening
to what one might say to a companion, who takes a swallow of cool wine as the
     man speaks,
and the waiter, full of tact, comes forward with the bottle precisely then, then with-
     draws.
How often they have felt the shapes that yearning and farewell take, the same few
     shapes.
After the table is set with precious ware, and sometimes strange—a marrow
     spoon,
a bowl of pepper (for intensities)—the guests arrive . . . ,
and the long, slow meal ends. How exposed their speeches and gestures.
How patient and unchanged the onlookers.

Six

Prodigal

They move now brimming with their own separate ways
together up the stairs at dusk. The days

are far removed, not hours and minutes but
what happens to things and animals, what

can't be helped. He turns to her smiling
darkly, harmed less by her remark (what was it?) than the nothing

to be done, and reaches to touch her hair;
nor does she find his gesture any less familiar

than before. And they press against each other—
a show of the summer softness—as if a little terror

could be pressed away by lips and arms. The breeze on
their faces cools, and there is no more reason

than in the night before to sense what the shadows have brought—
the feeling figure of themselves departing. They'd fought

and made up, but something overheard them—morose,
aloof, childish, full of sadnesses—and would not let it fall. Remorse-

less now, in *shudra* face and ashen brow,
it stands at the foot of the shadows

and waves good-bye—what was theirs and yet did not belong
to them. Sad nights that wait for the morning.

Dogs sleep in them, the flowers stand in them
in silent bunches while the winds carom.

Nor time nor change
shall ever change

them or their words. The next time they speak
in calmer tones, more or less deceit-

ful, standing before their house. The porch light
burns yellow, lonely and yellow the neighbor light,

while beyond its arc, the lost child wanders
and murmurs and ceases to remember.

Scorn

She thought of no wilder delicacy than the starling eggs she fed him for breakfast,
and if he sat and ate like a farmhand and she hated him sometimes,
she knew it didn't matter: that whatever in the din of argument
was harshly spoken, something else was done, soothed and patted away.
When they were young the towering fierceness
of their differences had frightened her even as she longed for physical release.
Out of their mouths such curses; their hands huge, pointing, stabbing the air.
How had they *not* been wounded? And wounded they'd convalesced in the same
    rooms
and bed. When at last they knew everything without confiding—fears, stinks,
boiling hearts—they gave up themselves a little so that they might both love and
    scorn
each other, and they ate from each other's hands.

Apology

Already the land is starting to forget gardens;
reminiscences no longer hold the heart completely
as someone held her a little roughly once in somber sweet groves,
and the touch she was utterly dissolute to, that caused collapse behind her knees,
sunslides in the lake, she feels a resistance toward, then apology,
as if a thorn catching her sweater has torn a small hole,—as if she shouldn't
have worn the sweater. What induces
then weakens the greater and lesser passions is what she'd like to know.
—Something like the green underneath red and yellow which is now wilting
has left her body; and she is someone who *had* loved
and is no longer availing and can neither take nor give away.

Seven

Farewell to Two Muses

Ah, Muse, I know you too well, your harp-song gets airy.
Carry me to hell,
deep into the kingdom of Dis where my love lies. What are his lyrics—
flesh and the paradisial snake? The nervous conscience, eternities of love
and guilt, evasions, a coldness of snow like sheets in summer?
Why won't you or he let more than these few words be spoken? You heard
his voice, mouth no longer kissed; irrevocably gone;
caught in a draft that blew in from a door, seeking to blow the heart out.
The lover moves only to be caught and let go; if he will listen, tell him this—
and in secret. Say to him his music like yours once brought us each to each.
And say if he asks who my lover is now, that I sleep alone; I have no other.

Self

They left her alone; it was what she wanted.
The bay waters had not been so secret for a long while, their great labor quiet.
She rowed over the calm of the ebb to an island of birds—heron, cormorant, egret
    waiting in the tall
mangroves, placid and self-contained, as if she alone were meant to see them
and find some meaning there. She back-watered through the down-strewn
    shallows
until one by one, then faster, all the birds rose, clucking, in some tribal crescendo.
    Immense cloud
heads stood close, above, like the whitened manes of blind and venerable gods,
gods, who remembering the fresh lands—now so remote—listened hard for the
    least shout
of anger or amazement. For a moment she felt she had pleased them,
though that hadn't been her intention, and no one else knew. But it remained in
    her:
what soared: the fierce rush: the birds crying fear: and herself the cause.

Former Beaus

This morning when I woke for the third or fourth time,
hungover with dream I watched the sun, cloud-laden,
struggling to stand. The arthritic shades and shadows
beneath the mangroves wavered as the wind
blew in from the bay. I wanted it to rain,
dissolve and rinse what seemed irremediable: Poor slain body,
a stranger will come to wash your face and limbs with a sponge.
If only beauty would die or be forgotten; and love (my former beaus).
But, transfigurable, they appear as on a banner of wings in air,
summer and winter: the baby-sized, gawky pelicans,
chins tucked down and turning their heads, that fly by.

Venus and Don Juan

She laid her forehead damp with salty water deep in the warmth of his wet chest,
   and he held her.
After all the ones to which they'd given themselves—that the fates seemed to
   choose—
there was this. In their affliction they spoke only of their own slow sweet moments
   in former days,
to tantalize and tear; or of all those others' hands, softskin, genitals; still relying on
   the senses, still refusing,
until she cried and felt her anger break into pieces so that her shyest places were
   exposed,
and his heart, which had been growing colder from the cold draught each day
   brought, and clearer,
clouded over and began to yield. Finding the other willing, and neglecting what
   those nearest would think,
they lovingly went forth and lost themselves:—once again pain and wildness,
   again the universe.
Later it would be said: Jealousy overcame them, snaring them in its net, laughing,
   piercing his side,
his slimness; lamentation to follow. But hadn't they rehearsed,
the pale moon slipping out of the sky each morning, doors shutting, the bed-
   clothes smoothed dry?
And what is left of their story but a fragment and the whispered expressions at
   midnight
of unheard ghosts who, with their own hearts in turmoil, have not wanted even
   this much told?

Notes

"Companion Of": The Hyatt grave is located in what is known as the Pope Cemetery, Otego, N.Y.

"Heart": Twelve emperors, sixteen empresses, Maria Theresa's nanny, and dozens of archdukes are entombed in the Kapuziner Church, but their hearts are in urns in the St. George Chapel of the Augustinerkirche in the Hofburg complex. Their entrails are similarly enshrined in a crypt below St. Stephan's Cathedral.

The details concerning mythic figures throughout the collection are adapted from various well-known sources (Edith Hamilton, Bulfinch, the Bible, etc.). Departures from the original are intentional.